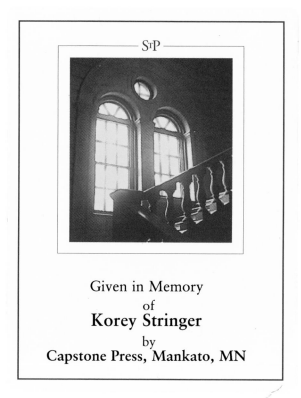

Learning about Cats

THE SPHYNX CAT

by Joanne Mattern

Consultant:
Kirsten Kranz
Cat Behaviorist/Purebred Cat Rescue
Cats International
Kenosha Humane Society, Wisconsin

CAPSTONE
HIGH-INTEREST
BOOKS

an imprint of Capstone Press
Mankato, Minnesota

Capstone High-Interest Books are published by Capstone Press
151 Good Counsel Drive, P.O. Box 669, Mankato, Minnesota 56002
http://www.capstone-press.com

Library of Congress Cataloging-in-Publication Data
Mattern, Joanne, 1963–
    The sphynx cat/by Joanne Mattern.
    p. cm.—(Learning about cats)
    Includes bibliographical references (p. 45) and index.
    ISBN 0-7368-0898-1
    I. Sphynx cat—Juvenile literature. [1. Sphynx cat. 2. Cats. 3. Pets.] I. Title.
II. Series.

SF449.S68 M37 2002
636.8—dc21   00-013079

Summary: Discusses the history, development, habits, and care of Sphynx cats.

Editorial Credits
Connie R. Colwell, editor; Lois Wallentine, product planning editor; Linda Clavel,
    cover designer and illustrator; Katy Kudela, photo researcher

Photo Credits
Chanan Photography, 15, 16, 20, 40–41
Kirsten Kranz, 24
Mark McCullough, 10, 26
Nancy M. McCallum, 4, 8, 18, 22, 28, 30, 33, 34, 36, 39
www.ronkimballstock.com, cover, 6, 12

1 2 3 4 5 6 07 06 05 04 03 02

Table of Contents

Quick Facts about the Sphynx

Description

Size: Sphynx cats have lean, muscular bodies. They are medium-sized cats.

Weight: Most male Sphynx weigh between 8 and 10 pounds (3.6 and 4.5 kilograms). Most females weigh between 6 and 8 pounds (2.7 and 3.6 kilograms).

Physical features: Sphynx cats have almost no fur. They have very large ears and large,

4

oval-shaped eyes. Sphynx cats have wedge-shaped heads.

Colors: Sphynx cats can be many colors. These colors include white, black, brown, and red.

Development
Place of origin: The first Sphynx cat was found in Ontario, Canada.

History of breed: In 1966, a Canadian cat gave birth to a hairless kitten. Later, a cat in Minnesota and another cat in Toronto, Canada, each gave birth to several hairless kittens. These kittens were the first Sphynx.

Numbers: In 2000, the Cat Fanciers' Association (CFA) registered 120 Sphynx cats. Owners who register their purebred cats record the cats' breeding records with an official club. The CFA is the largest organization of cat breeders in the world. But The International Cat Association (TICA) registers more Sphynx than the CFA. In 2000, TICA registered 622 Sphynx.

Chapter 1

The Sphynx Cat

The Sphynx is one of the most unusual cat breeds. Sphynx cats' almost hairless bodies give them an appearance unlike cats of any other breed.

Appearance

Sphynx are medium-sized cats. Their bodies are lean and muscular. Most males weigh between 8 and 10 pounds (3.6 and 4.5 kilograms). Females are smaller. Most females weigh between 6 and 8 pounds (2.7 and 3.6 kilograms).

Sphynx cats often are called hairless cats. But Sphynx do have hair. Very short, fine hairs called down cover the Sphynx's body. The down may be slightly longer on the cat's ears, nose, tail, and paws.

Sphynx cats have almost hairless bodies.

Sphynx cats have very large ears.

The Sphynx's down makes its body feel different to the touch than other cats. Some people say that the Sphynx feels like a soft piece of cloth called suede. Others think it feels like a warm peach.

Sphynx cats also have unusual faces. They have a narrow, pointed face that is shaped like a wedge. This shape looks like an upside-down triangle. Sphynx cats have very large ears and large, oval-shaped eyes.

Sphynx cats do not have long, straight whiskers like most other cats do. Instead, some Sphynx's whiskers are short and curly. Many Sphynx do not have any whiskers at all.

Personality

Sphynx are affectionate cats. They seem to enjoy being around people and other animals. They also seem to enjoy being the center of attention.

Sphynx cats are very active. They have a great deal of energy. They seem to enjoy playing, running, and climbing.

Sphynx cats tend to make good family pets. They get along well with children. They also get along well with dogs and other cats. They seem to prefer homes with other pets to keep them company.

People often believe that Sphynx cats make good pets for people who are allergic to cats. Some people who are allergic to cat hair can have a Sphynx as a pet. But Sphynx cats' skin still produces flakes called dander. People who are allergic to cat dander may still have an allergic reaction to Sphynx cats. People who are allergic to cats should spend some time around a Sphynx before adopting the cat as a pet.

Chapter 2

Development of the Breed

The Sphynx breed developed in the 1960s. It is one of the world's newest cat breeds.

The History of Hairless Cats

Hairless cats have been born throughout history. But records of these cats did not begin until the early 1900s. About 1903, two hairless cats were born in New Mexico. The owners did not breed these cats because they were brother and sister. The cats were called New Mexican Hairless cats. They are not related to today's Sphynx.

Today's Sphynx cat breed began by accident in 1966. A black-and-white pet cat in Ontario, Canada, gave birth to a hairless kitten. The owner named the kitten Prune because of its hairless, wrinkled skin. Prune's owner bred him to try to create more hairless kittens. Some of

The first Sphynx cats occurred by accident.

Devon Rex cats were bred to hairless cats to create the Sphynx breed.

the resulting kittens had hair. Others were hairless. Some people called these kittens Canadian Hairless Cats. Others called them Sphynx cats. They thought these cats looked like an ancient Egyptian cat sculpture called the Sphinx.

These early hairless kittens had serious health problems. They did not develop healthy immune systems. Cats' immune systems help protect them from diseases. It was not safe or popular to breed more of these cats. For a time, it looked like the breed would not continue.

In 1975, a cat in Wadena, Minnesota, produced several hairless kittens. One of these kittens was named Epidermis. Epidermis was bred to other cats to create a new line of hairless kittens. Epidermis became one of the most important cats in Sphynx history.

In 1978, three hairless kittens were found on the streets in Toronto, Canada. One kitten was male and two were female. The male kitten was named Bambi. The females were named Punkie and Paloma. Bambi stayed in Canada. But the two females were sent to Doctor Hugo Hernandez in the Netherlands. Hernandez was a cat breeder. He used Punkie and Paloma to begin a line of European Sphynx cats. Hernandez bred the cats to a male Devon Rex. The Devon Rex is another cat breed that has very little body hair. Today, some offspring of these European Sphynx cats live in North America.

The Sphynx Cat's Genes

The Sphynx's lack of body hair is the result of genes. Genes are parts of cells in the body that carry messages about how an animal's body will look. Kittens receive some genes from their mother and some genes from their father. These genes give cats their eye color, body size, and gender.

Sphynx cats receive two genes that cause them to be hairless. These genes are recessive. Recessive genes are weaker than other genes. Cats with furry coats sometimes carry one recessive gene for hairlessness. But they have another gene that gives them hair. Cats must receive a recessive hairless gene from each parent to be hairless.

Two furry cats that each carry one gene for hairlessness sometimes mate. Some of the kittens from this match may receive both recessive genes. These kittens will be hairless.

Cats' whiskers also are hairs. The genes for hairlessness prevent Sphynx cats' whiskers from growing long and straight. These genes sometimes cause Sphynx to have no whiskers at all.

Recognizing the Breed

Several cat associations are located in North America. It takes time for a new breed to be

Sphynx kittens receive genes for hairlessness from their parents.

recognized by these cat associations. Breeds that are recognized by these associations can appear in cat shows sponsored by the associations.

At first, only The International Cat Association (TICA) recognized the Sphynx. Sphynx cats could only appear at TICA shows.

Later, other cat associations recognized the Sphynx. In 1998, the Cat Fanciers' Association (CFA) recognized the Sphynx. The CFA is the largest organization of cat breeders in the world.

Chapter 3

Today's Sphynx

Today's Sphynx cats are free of the immune system problems of early Sphynx. Sphynx can be healthy cats if they are bred carefully.

Today's Sphynx are friendly, intelligent cats. They are muscular and playful. They seem to like being around people and other animals. They also seem to enjoy cuddling.

Sphynx cats can be different colors and color patterns. People can tell a Sphynx cat's color by looking at its skin. Some of these colors and color patterns include white, black, red, brown, calico, and tortoiseshell. Calico cats have patches of white, black, and red. Tortoiseshell cats are black and red with few or no white markings.

Sphynx cats can be different colors and color patterns.

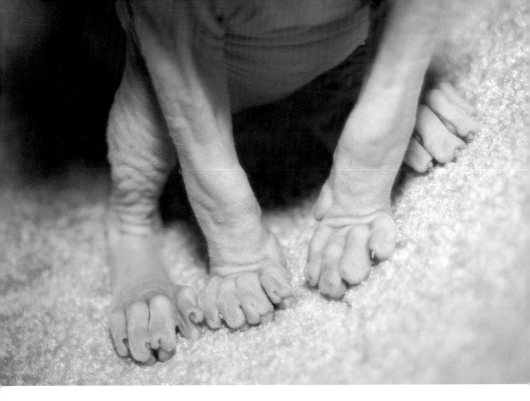

Sphynx cats should have long toes.

Breed Standard

Sphynx cats may compete in the miscellaneous
category at CFA shows. Cats in this category
cannot earn any awards. But people still can
exhibit their Sphynx cats at these shows.

Judges look for certain physical features
when they are judging a Sphynx in a cat show.
These features are called the breed standard.

The general breed standard says the Sphynx's body should be slender and muscular. Sphynx cats' legs should be slim and sturdy. They should have a round stomach. But they should not be fat. Their stomachs should look as though they just ate a meal.

The Sphynx's paws should be large and round. They should have long toes. The toes may have some hair on them.

A Sphynx's tail should be thin and long like a whip. Sphynx cats may have a puff of hair at the end of their tail.

The Sphynx's skin should be wrinkled and should feel like suede. There should be very little hair on the body.

The Sphynx's head should be long and wedge-shaped. The cat's ears should be very large. The inside of the ears should be completely hairless. Sphynx may have some hair on the outside of their ears. Their eyes must be large, wide apart, and oval-shaped.

Chapter 4

Owning a Sphynx

People interested in adopting a Sphynx should contact a breeder. People often contact animal shelters, breed rescue organizations, or pet stores when they are looking for cats to adopt. But Sphynx cats are rare. Most animal shelters, breed rescue organizations, and pet stores do not have Sphynx available.

Finding a Sphynx through a Breeder
People who want a show-quality or good pet-quality Sphynx should buy one from a breeder. These people carefully breed their cats to make sure they are healthy and meet the breed standard. People who buy a kitten from a breeder often can meet the kitten's parents. This meeting gives owners an idea

The best place to adopt a good pet-quality Sphynx is from a breeder.

People may have to wait before adopting a Sphynx.

of how the kitten will look and behave when grown.

Sphynx cat breeders live in the United States and Canada. People who want to find a local Sphynx breeder can attend cat shows. Cat shows are good places to talk to breeders and see their cats.

Many breeders advertise in newspapers and cat magazines. Breeders also can be found on the Internet. People should visit breeders before they adopt a cat. During the visit, people should ask the breeders for names and telephone numbers of people who have bought cats from these breeders. They should ask for the medical history of the breeders' cats. Good breeders do not sell kittens under 12 weeks of age.

Some Sphynx breeders may ask buyers for references. These breeders want to make sure their Sphynx are going to good homes. Breeders may ask buyers to sign papers stating that they will not have their Sphynx's claws removed. They also may ask buyers to sign papers stating that they will not allow their Sphynx cats outside.

People may have to wait before adopting a Sphynx. Sphynx cats are rare. Sphynx breeders often have waiting lists. Breeders put people's names on waiting lists. They then contact the people when a Sphynx cat or kitten becomes available.

Breed rescue organizations often have mixed-breed cats available for adoption.

Breed Rescue Organizations

People interested in adopting a Sphynx may want to contact a breed rescue organization. Breed rescue organization members find unwanted or neglected animals of certain breeds. They care for the animals and try to find new homes for them.

Sphynx cats are rare. Breed rescue
organizations rescue few of these cats.
But people can contact these organizations.
They can ask to be put on a waiting list.
Organization workers will contact these
people if a Sphynx becomes available.

Adopting a Sphynx from a breed rescue
organization can have some advantages
over adopting from breeders. Breed rescue
organizations are less expensive than breeders.
People who adopt from these organizations
also may enjoy giving homeless cats new
places to live.

People can find information about breed
rescue organizations in several ways. These
organizations often have their own Internet
sites. They also may advertise in newspapers
or cat magazines. Breeders and workers at
animal shelters also may refer people to
breed rescue organizations.

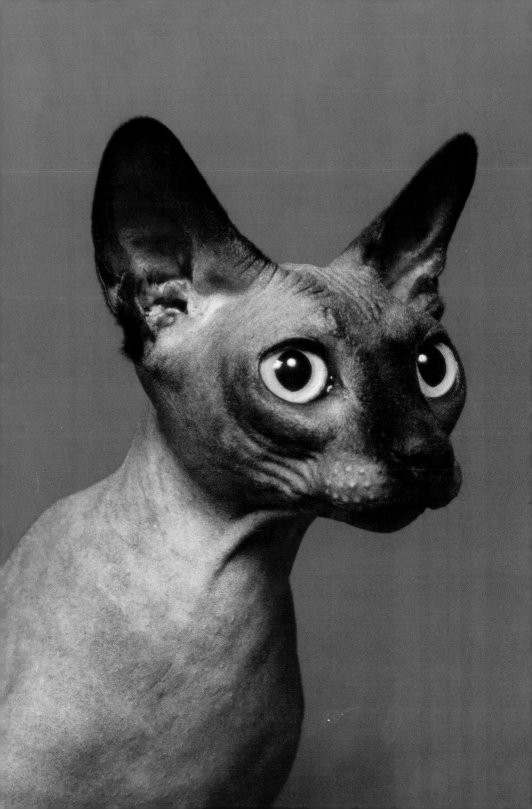

Chapter 5

Caring for a Sphynx

Sphynx are strong cats. Healthy Sphynx may live 15 years or longer with good care.

Feeding

Sphynx need high-quality cat food. Sphynx cats have a fast metabolism. A cat's metabolism is the rate that it changes food into energy. Many quality cat foods in supermarkets or pet stores provide a balanced, healthy diet for Sphynx cats.

Some cat owners feed their cats dry food. This food usually is less expensive than other types of food. Dry food also can help keep cats' teeth clean. It will not spoil if it is left in a dish.

Healthy Sphynx may live 15 years or longer.

27

Other owners feed their cats moist, canned food. This type of food will spoil if it is left out for more than one hour. Owners who feed their cats moist food usually feed their adult cats twice each day. The amount of food needed depends on the individual cat.

Both dry food and moist food can be suitable for Sphynx cats. Different cats may prefer different types of food. Owners can ask a veterinarian for advice on which type of cat food is best.

Cats need to drink water to stay healthy. Owners should make sure their cats' bowls always are filled with fresh, clean water. Owners should replace the water in the bowls each day.

Indoor and Outdoor Cats

Some cat owners allow their cats to roam outdoors. But Sphynx cats should never go outside. Cats that roam outdoors are at a much greater risk for disease than cats that are kept indoors. Outdoor cats also face dangers from

Sphynx cats need to sharpen their claws on scratching posts.

Owners of Sphynx cats need to provide their cats with at least one large litter box.

cars and other animals. Sphynx cats do not have much fur to keep them warm or protect them from the sun. Their skin easily can freeze or burn outdoors. Owners should keep Sphynx cats inside where the temperature is not too hot or too cold.

Owners of indoor cats need to provide their cats with at least one large litter box. Owners fill the box with small bits of clay called litter.

Cats eliminate waste in litter boxes. Owners should clean the waste out of the box each day and change the litter often. Cats are clean animals. They may refuse to use a dirty litter box.

All cats need to scratch. Cats mark their territories by leaving their scent on objects they scratch. Cats also scratch to release tension and keep their claws sharp. This habit can be a problem if cats choose to scratch on furniture, carpet, or curtains. Owners should provide their cats with a scratching post. They can buy a scratching post at a pet store. Owners also can make one from wood and rope. Scratching posts at least 3 feet (.9 meters) tall work best.

Sphynx cats are playful and energetic cats. They may destroy furniture or other objects if they become bored. People should purchase cat toys or a cat tree to keep their Sphynx busy. Cats climb and play on cat trees. These structures often are made of wood and carpet.

Grooming

Sphynx cats have little fur. But they still need to be groomed. Cats' coats usually absorb the oils from their skin. But a Sphynx must be bathed regularly to keep its skin free of oils. Owners should use special shampoo made for cats. This shampoo is available at most pet stores.

Cats usually do not like to be bathed. It is important to begin bathing a Sphynx when it is a kitten. The kitten will become used to taking baths. It also is important to rub Sphynx cats every day with a damp, soft cloth to absorb body oil.

The Sphynx's ears require special care. The hair inside cats' ears usually helps keep dirt and wax out. But Sphynx's ears are hairless and very large. The insides of their ears can get dirty and full of dust. Owners should wipe out their cats' ears with a soft, wet washcloth or a damp cotton ball.

The tip of a cat's claw is called the nail. Sphynx cats need their nails trimmed every few weeks. Trimming helps reduce damage if

Sphynx cats need help grooming themselves.

cats scratch on the carpet or furniture. It also protects cats from infections caused by ingrown nails. Infections can occur when a cat seldom sharpens its claws. The claws then grow into the bottom of the paw.

Owners should use a special nail clipper to trim their cats' nails. Veterinarians can show owners the proper way to trim their cats' nails. It

Owners should trim their Sphynx's nails every few weeks.

is best to begin trimming a cat's nails when it is a kitten. The kitten will become used to having its nails trimmed as it grows older.

Dental Care

Sphynx cats need regular dental care to protect their teeth and gums from plaque. This coating of bacteria and saliva causes tooth decay and gum disease. Dry cat food helps remove plaque from cats' teeth. Owners also should brush their cats' teeth at least once each week. They can use a toothbrush made for cats or a soft cloth. Owners should use toothpaste made for cats to brush the cats' teeth. Cats become sick if they swallow toothpaste that is made for people.

Brushing may not be enough to remove the plaque from older cats' teeth. These cats may need to have their teeth cleaned once each year by a veterinarian.

Health Problems

Early Sphynx cats sometimes had unhealthy immune systems. Their weak immune systems did not protect them from illnesses. But these problems are not present in today's Sphynx cats. Most people agree that Sphynx cats are as healthy as any other cat breed.

Cats sometimes have diseases that are passed down from their parents. Good cat

Some owners feed their cats a mixture of moist and dry food. Dry cat food helps keep Sphynx cats' teeth clean.

breeders test their animals for these diseases. They do not breed animals that suffer from serious illnesses. Breeders should have information on their cats' medical histories. People should review this information when choosing a Sphynx cat.

Veterinarian Visits

Sphynx cats must visit a veterinarian regularly for checkups. Most veterinarians recommend yearly visits for cats. Older cats may need to visit the veterinarian two or three times each year. Older cats often have health problems.

Owners should take their Sphynx to the veterinarian for a checkup as soon as they adopt the cat. The veterinarian will check the cat's heart, lungs, internal organs, eyes, ears, mouth, and coat.

The veterinarian also will give the Sphynx vaccinations. These shots of medicine help prevent serious diseases. Serious cat diseases include rabies, feline panleukopenia, and feline leukemia. Cats also can be vaccinated against several respiratory diseases that cause breathing or lung problems. These diseases include the rhinostracheitis virus, the calici virus, and chlamydia psittaci.

Rabies is a deadly disease that is spread by animal bites. Most states and provinces have laws that require owners to vaccinate their cats against rabies.

Feline panleukopenia also is called feline distemper. This virus causes fever, vomiting, and death. Owners who bring their cats to shows often vaccinate their cats for feline leukemia. This disease attacks a cat's immune system. Feline leukemia is spread from cat to cat by bodily fluids.

Cats should receive some vaccinations each year. Others are given less often. Breeders have information on which vaccinations Sphynx cats need. Owners should keep a record of the dates vaccines are given to their cats. This helps owners make sure that their cats have received all the necessary vaccinations.

Veterinarians also spay female cats and neuter male cats. These surgeries make it impossible for cats to breed. Owners who are not planning to breed their cats should have them spayed or neutered. These surgeries keep unwanted kittens from being born. They also

People who own Sphynx cats appreciate the breed as an intelligent, friendly companion.

help prevent diseases such as infections and cancers of the reproductive organs. Spayed and neutered cats usually have calmer personalities than cats that are not spayed or neutered. They also are less likely to wander away from home.

The Sphynx may not look like other cats. But people who own Sphynx cats appreciate the breed as an intelligent, friendly companion.

Ears

Paws

Markings

Tail

Quick Facts about Cats

A male cat is called a tom. A female cat is called a queen. A young cat is called a kitten. A family of kittens born at one time is called a litter.

Origin: Shorthaired cat breeds descended from a type of African wildcat called *Felis lybica*. Longhaired breeds may have descended from Asian wildcats. People domesticated or tamed these breeds as early as 1500 B.C.

Types: The Cat Fanciers' Association accepts 40 domestic cat breeds for competition. The smallest breeds weigh about 5 to 7 pounds (2.3 to 3.2 kilograms) when grown. The largest breeds can weigh more than 18 pounds (8.2 kilograms). Cat breeds may be either shorthaired or longhaired. Cats' coats can be a variety of colors. These colors include many shades of white, black, gray, brown, and red.

Reproduction: Most cats are sexually mature at 5 or 6 months. A sexually mature female cat goes into estrus several times each year. Estrus also is called "heat." During this time, she can mate with a male. Kittens are born about 65 days after breeding. An average litter includes four kittens.

Development: Kittens are born blind and deaf. Their eyes open about 10 days after birth. Their hearing develops at the same time. They can live on their own when they are 6 weeks old.

Life span: With good care, cats can live 15 or more years.

Sight: A cat's eyesight is adapted for hunting. Cats are good judges of distance. They see movement more easily than detail. Cats also have excellent night vision.

Hearing: Cats can hear sounds that are too high for humans to hear. A cat can turn its ears to focus on different sounds.

Smell: A cat has an excellent sense of smell. Cats use scents to establish their territories. Cats scratch or rub the sides of their faces against objects. These actions release a scent from glands between their toes or in their skin.

Taste: Cats cannot taste as many foods as people can. For example, cats are not very sensitive to sweet tastes.

Touch: Cats' whiskers are sensitive to touch. Cats use their whiskers to touch objects and sense changes in their surroundings.

Balance: Cats have an excellent sense of balance. They use their tails to help keep their balance. Cats can walk on narrow objects without falling. They usually can right themselves and land on their feet during falls from short distances.

Communication: Cats use many sounds to communicate with people and other animals. They may meow when hungry or hiss when afraid. Cats also purr. Scientists do not know exactly what causes cats to make this sound. Cats often purr when they are relaxed. But they also may purr when they are sick or in pain.

Words to Know

breeder (BREED-ur)—someone who breeds and raises cats or other animals

breed standard (BREED STAN-durd)—certain physical features in a breed that judges look for at a cat show

estrus (ESS-truss)—a physical state of a female cat during which she will mate with a male cat; estrus also is known as "heat."

neuter (NOO-tur)—to remove a male animal's testicles so that it cannot reproduce

spay (SPAY)—to remove a female animal's uterus and ovaries so that it cannot reproduce

vaccination (vak-suh-NAY-shun)—a shot of medicine that protects an animal from disease

veterinarian (vet-ur-uh-NER-ee-uhn)—a doctor who is trained to treat the illnesses and injuries of animals

To Learn More

Petras, Kathryn, and Ross Petras. *Cats: 47 Favorite Breeds, Appearance, History, Personality and Lore.* Fandex Family Field Guides. New York: Workman Publishing, 1997.

Quasha, Jennifer. *The Sphynx: The Hairless Cat.* Kid's Cat Library. New York: PowerKids Press, 2000.

You can read articles about Sphynx cats in *Cat Fancy* and *Cats* magazines.

Useful Addresses

Canadian Cat Association (CCA)
289 Rutherford Road South
Unit 18
Brampton, ON L6W 3R9
Canada

The Cat Fanciers' Association (CFA)
P.O. Box 1005
Manasquan, NJ 08736-0805

The International Cat Association (TICA)
P.O. Box 2684
Harlingen, TX 78551

Progressive Sphynx Alliance
246 Leonard Road
Rochester, NY 14616

Internet Sites

Canadian Cat Association (CCA)
http://www.cca-afc.com

The Cat Fanciers' Association (CFA)
http://www.cfainc.org

Cats International
http://www.catsinternational.org

The International Cat Association (TICA)
http://www.tica.org

**International Sphynx Breeders and
    Fanciers Association**
http://www.sphynx.org

Index